Chick-Chick the Ping-Pong Champ

by Russell Ginns
illustrated by Ethan Long

Hush! We will now begin the story of a grand champ.

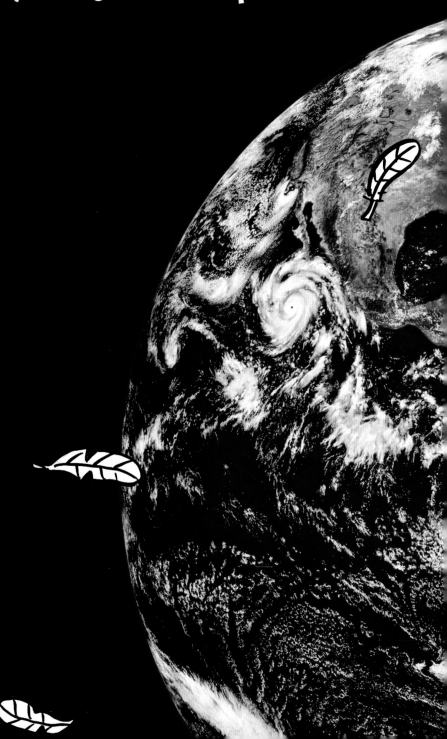

No. This is not the tale of
Ken Ben Bumplump of Dublin.
He was the first man to hop
on one leg for ten long days.

And no . . . this is not about Jill Mill Mumpdump. She was the first kid to run across Finland. And she did it with six pigs on her back!

This champ happens to be better than Ken Ben and Jill Mill and Kip Flip Grumpstump. (And you do not want to know all the things that Kip Flip Grumpstump did.)

This champ was at the top of her game. She was first class. She went all over the world to show us what it is like to be a hero. She was . . .

. . . Chick-Chick,
the Ping-Pong champ!

Chick-Chick was hatched out West. From the first day Chick-Chick could flap her wings, she had a skill. She could hit any rock or egg she could see.

Then Farmer Matchpatch said, "Chick-Chick, you are a whiz. I want you to go out and play Ping-Pong. You can be a champ. And I want you to stop hitting the eggs!"

So Chick-Chick went out to play.

She went all over the USA.

14

She was a smash hit.

She was the new Ping-Pong champ!

Then Chick-Chick went to France.
The top Ping-Pong player in the land
was quick. But she was not so quick
that she could stop Chick-Chick.

Then Chick-Chick went to play a match with two men in India.

They were top-notch, but they swung and they swung. They could not smack the ball when Chick-Chick hit it.

19

It was time for the grand match.
Chick-Chick went to China.

The Ping-Pong champ in that land was **Ling-Ling**.

They went slam and wham.

They went swing and fling.

They went crash and smash.
What a match!

In the end, Ling-Ling was
the champ of the world.

"That's the way it goes," said Ling-Ling. "You do not have to be sad. I bet you will make a great chess champ."

Handbook of Latinos and Education

Providing a comprehensive review of rigorous, innovative, and critical scholarship relevant to educational issues which impact Latinos, this *Handbook* captures the field at this point in time. Its unique purpose and function is to profile the scope and terrain of academic inquiry on Latinos and education. Presenting the most significant and potentially influential work in the field in terms of its contributions to research, to professional practice, and to the emergence of related interdisciplinary studies and theory, the volume is organized around five themes:

- History, Theory, and Methodology
- Policies and Politics
- Language and Culture
- Teaching and Learning
- Resources and Information

The *Handbook of Latinos and Education* is a must-have resource for educational researchers, graduate students, teacher educators, and the broad spectrum of individuals, groups, agencies, organizations, and institutions sharing a common interest in and commitment to the educational issues that impact Latinos.

Enrique G. Murillo, Jr. is Associate Professor in the department of Language, Literacy, and Culture at California State University, San Bernardino.

Sofia A. Villenas is Associate Professor of Education and Director of the Latino/a Studies Program at Cornell University.

Ruth Trinidad Galván is Assistant Professor in the Language, Literacy, and Sociocultural Studies Department at the University of New Mexico.

Juan Sánchez Muñoz is Associate Professor in the Department of Curriculum and Instruction and Director of the Center for Research in Leadership and Education, in the College of Education, Texas Tech University.

Corinne Martínez is Associate Professor in the Department of Teacher Education at California State University, Long Beach.

Margarita Machado-Casas is Assistant Professor in the Department of Bicultural Bilingual Studies at the University of Texas at San Antonio.